DOGS
LOOK-AND-LEARN
by DR. HERBERT RICHARDS

PHOTO CREDITS

All photos by Isabelle Francais, the world's leading canine photographer. Ms. Francais has illustrated more dog books than any other dog photographer. Additional photos have been supplied by Vince Serbin.

The products shown in this book are known to be safe and effective. They are available at most pet shops. The Gumabone® Frisbee® shown here has a bone on top so the dog can grasp it when it lies flat on a smooth surface.

Distributed in the UNITED STATES to the Pet Trade by T.F.H. Publications, Inc., One T.F.H. Plaza, Neptune City, NJ 07753; distributed in the UNITED STATES to the Bookstore and Library Trade by National Book Network, Inc. 4720 Boston Way, Lanham MD 20706; in CANADA to the Pet Trade by H & L Pet Supplies Inc., 27 Kingston Crescent, Kitchener, Ontario N2B 2T6; Rolf C. Hagen Ltd., 3225 Sartelon Street, Montreal 382 Quebec; in CANADA to the Book Trade by Macmillan of Canada (A Division of Canada Publishing Corporation), 164 Commander Boulevard, Agincourt, Ontario M1S 3C7; in the United Kingdom by T.F.H. Publications, PO Box 15, Waterlooville PO7 6BQ; in AUSTRALIA AND THE SOUTH PACIFIC by T.F.H. (Australia), Pty. Ltd., Box 149, Brookvale 2100 N.S.W., Australia; in NEW ZEALAND by Brooklands Aquarium Ltd. 5 McGiven Drive, New Plymouth, RD1 New Zealand; in Japan by T.F.H. Publications, Japan—Jiro Tsuda, 10-12-3 Ohjidai, Sakura, Chiba 285, Japan; in SOUTH AFRICA by Multipet Pty. Ltd., P.O. Box 35347, Northway, 4065, South Africa. Published by T.F.H. Publications, Inc.

Manufactured in the United States of America by T.F.H. Publications, Inc.

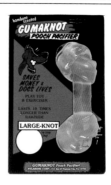

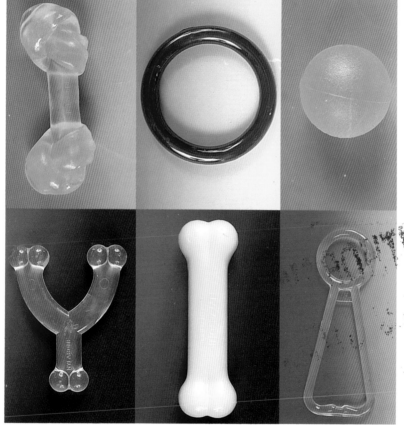

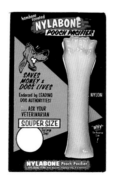

Your local pet shop carries Nylabone®, Gumabone® and Flexibone® dog pacifiers. These are highly recommended to satisfy your dog's natural chewing desires. I recommend Nylabone® products because they are the only chew products for dog's which have been scientifically tested and proven effective in the control of tartar and tooth decay in dogs. There have been many copies of Nylabone® products but these have had to be changed to skirt Nylabone®'s patents and trademarks. None of these copies have been scientifically proven to be effective. Therefore, the author has no qualms about wholeheartedly recommending Nylabone® products for your dog.

Nylabone®, Gumabone® and *Flexibone®* are registered tradenames and are used here with permission and they are accepted for advertising in veterinary medicine journals.

CARE

Pet shops carry most of your dog's needs. I recommend pet stores because they give you free valuable advice along with the products they sell. They also stand behind their products should anything be faulty or incorrect (like the wrong size collar).

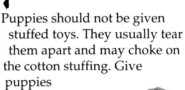

Puppies should not be given stuffed toys. They usually tear them apart and may choke on the cotton stuffing. Give puppies veterinarian-recommended Nylabone®, Gumabone® or Flexibone® dental devices.

← Dog muzzles are required by law under certain circumstances. Muzzles prevent dogs from biting.

Dog harnesses are more humane than collars. Make sure they fit loosely but not so loose that the dog can slip out of them.

The Nylabone® Frisbee® has been made especially strong for dogs. The bone on the top enables the dog to pick it up (think about how difficult it would be for a dog to pick up a Frisbee® from the sidewalk where there is no space under the Frisbee® to get a grip). The Gumabone® Frisbee® is soft and is recommended for throwing on the beach or where it might strike people or glass. The Gumabone® Frisbee® is soft enough to fold up.

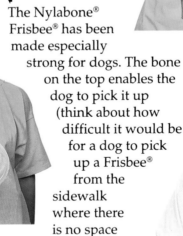

Children should be taught to keep their dogs immaculately groomed. If brushing becomes a daily habit, your home will be spared loose hairs on the furniture and carpets.

This Border Collie enjoys his Gumabone® Frisbee®. Be careful when using any throw device. It might land on grass which might have been treated with fertilizer or herbicide. Sterilize (by boiling for 20 minutes) as often as possible; or put it into your dish washer with the dishes. Only Nylabone®, Gumabone® and Flexibone® Frisbees® can be sterilized; other brands might melt! If in doubt check with the manufacturer or the store where you bought it.

Retractable leads allow you to control how far you want your dog to run ahead of you. The length of the lead is adjustable. Pet shops carry several brands.

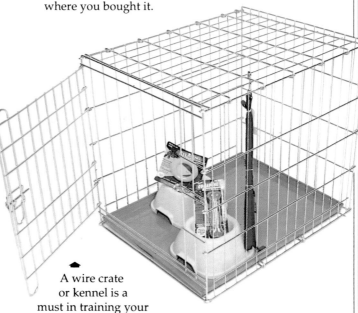

A wire crate or kennel is a must in training your dog. It is also necessary for travelling and for restraining your dog for its protection. It comes in handy, too, when you want to leave your house open. These kennels come in different sizes. Be sure to keep food, water and a chew device available in the kennel at all times.

Never feed your dog from the table when you are eating! Your dog should be offered premium dog food (usually available at your local pet shop) in a clean dog dish.

Your local pet shop will usually have a supply of grooming accessories which are necessary for the health of your dog's skin and coat. Get into the habit of grooming your dog daily.

Four Paws® makes an excellent grooming device called a Shed'n Blade®. It comes in various sizes for every dog. Use it to remove dead hairs, knots and tangles. It is a simple device, very effective and reasonably priced.

CARE

If you cannot or will not properly care for a puppy, you should not have one. Puppies need exercise, friendship, training and proper equipment to keep them safe, healthy and busy. On these pages are the bare essentials.

◀ Nylon ropes, sometimes referred to as *bones,* are knotted and flavored. They should be sterilized or thrown in with your laundry once a week or more. DO NOT USE COTTON ROPES. The dogs can choke on them, as they come apart easily.

◀ This black Labrador Retriever has been using a Nylafloss® for training. It has the advantage of being a very effective dental device. Made of nylon like human dental floss, a properly sized Nylafloss® can last a very long time. If the dog opens the knot, get a new one.

◀

If your dog scratches continually, it is a sign of parasites or skin problems (like allergies). Your pet shop has several over-the-counter flea and tick sprays and medicated shampoos. If these don't work immediately, take your dog to a veterinarian.

◀ Leather or nylon leads are essentials for walking with and training your dog. Training must start at an early age. *You can't teach an old dog new tricks* is a saying that is not too far from correct. Your local pet shop can match up the lead with your dog's needs.

Chain collars and leads are also available. I do NOT recommend choke collars for pet dogs. They may be acceptable under certain conditions such as when a dog is a problem when walking on a lead and must be restrained from pulling you along the sidewalk. ▼

◀ This Australian Shepherd puppy has a Flexibone® which is too large for it now, but will be the correct size in a few months. Puppies must chew in order to help their teeth develop; they also have a natural tendency to chew. If you don't give them a proper dental device they'll chew anything available including furniture.

▲This lucky Australian Shepherd puppy has Flexibones to play with. These are just the right size. It is important that you get the correct size of dental devices for your puppy.

◀ Big dogs with strong jaws should NOT be given small, soft dental devices. Only the largest and strongest devices are suitable for breeds over 60 pounds or with strong jaws. Such a device is the Gumabone® Plaque Attacker shown below.

▶ A Golden Retriever with a properly sized Nylabone® product. Retrievers are natural retrieving animals. They also like to swim but don't give them a floating chew device because they are too weak and the dog can easily chew them up and perhaps swallow some of the smaller pieces.

◀Perhaps the best chew device in the world (especially for larger dogs) is the Gumabone® Plaque Attacker. It helps keep a dog's teeth clean and it is safe, being too large and too hard for the usual dog to tear apart. Your dog's teeth, like your own, should be examined and treated by a professional regularly. Chew devices only HELP, they don't CURE.

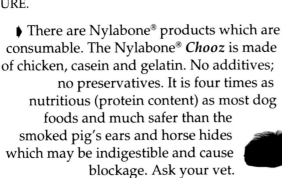

▶ There are Nylabone® products which are consumable. The Nylabone® *Chooz* is made of chicken, casein and gelatin. No additives; no preservatives. It is four times as nutritious (protein content) as most dog foods and much safer than the smoked pig's ears and horse hides which may be indigestible and cause blockage. Ask your vet.

BREEDING

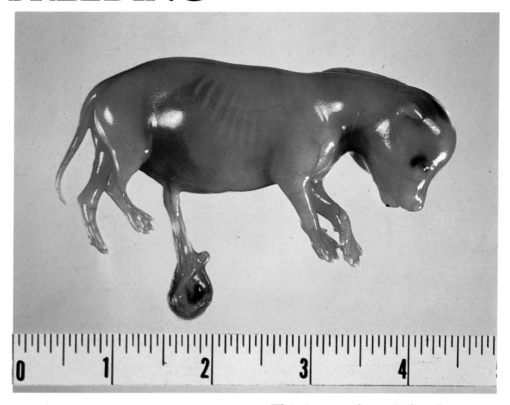

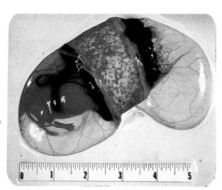

◄ This is an unborn Labrador Retriever about half of term. The characteristics which determine the so-called *quality* of a dog are passed on from generation to generation by their parents. These genetic traits are governed by Mendelian laws which allow us to predict certain aspects of progeny produced by parents with known genetic structures.

◄ Dogs develop in a manner similar to humans. The puppies develop as aquatic animals in liquid-containing sacs which protect the developing embryo.

▶ Dogs differ from humans by almost always having multiple births produced by the female's having more than one egg available for fertilization at the same time. Each lump is an unborn Labrador Retriever. The specimens shown here were taken from a road-death pregnant female.

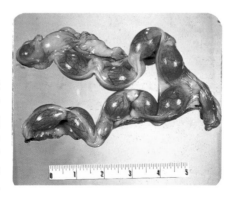

The skulls shown above are from different types of dogs. All of these dogs are the same scientific species and the skulls have evolved by selective breeding through many generations. The normal bite, *above right*, could be a Dachshund; the upper left skull could have been any undershot dog like a Boston Terrier. The lower skull is a dog with a very protrusive lower jaw like a bulldog-type. The development of a show-quality dog, like the Greyhound shown to the left, takes many generations of breeding with selection of the parents done according to strict standards.

Affenpinscher

◀ AFFENPINSCHER

This dog was developed in Germany more than 300 years ago. It weighs about 7-8 pounds and stays about 10 inches in height. The coat is medium long, very wiry and not too pleasant to the touch. The preferred color is black but black/tan, red, or dark gray are also recognized for show purposes. The coat requires daily brushing. The Affenpinscher makes an excellent pet.

➤ AFGHAN HOUND

This dog was developed in Afghanistan so long ago that the local people claim this to be the dog that Noah took into his Ark before the Great Flood. It is a large dog growing to 27 inches at the shoulder. It weighs up to 60 pounds. Heavier dogs are very undesirable and lose that sleek look for which Afghans are noted. These are aloof and intelligent dogs and not for the beginner.

AIREDALE TERRIER ▶

This dog was developed in Great Britain, probably in the early 1800s. They are a very frisky dog which reach about 44 pounds and almost two feet at the shoulder. They are black and tan and saddled, which means they must be marked with black as though it were a saddle. The coat is wiry, hard, and stiff. This is a terrier which needs lots of exercise to be kept in prime condition.

American Foxhound

AKITA ▶

This dog was developed in Japan hundreds of years ago. It may have been originally bred for its fighting ability. Being a Northern breed, it can stand a lot of cold, as its thick coat and undercoat reflect. The dog can reach 110 pounds with a shoulder height of 28 inches. It comes in all colors including solid white, pied or brindle. It is not an especially friendly dog, being more a *one-man dog.*

◆ ALASKAN MALAMUTE

This dog is one of the oldest breeds having been used by the Northern people since the Stone Age. They are beasts of burden. They drag sleds and carry heavy loads in saddles over their backs. They are very hardy and can live in snow and sleep on ice. They were once fed frozen fish. In many Alaskan environments they are the only domesticated animal that can survive. They reach 85 pounds at 25 inches shoulder height. They are basically black with various gray shades. They carry their tail curled over their backs like most Oriental breeds.

◆ AMERICAN FOXHOUND

This dog derives from the grand fox-hunting hound dogs of Great Britain. It is a good-size dog, standing between 22 and 25 inches. The coat is short and dense and always colored in a two or three color pattern. Foxhounds most commonly are brown, black and white. This is a hardy hunting dog that loves people and other dogs. Not too usually kept as a pet, the American Foxhound offers much as a family dog.

American Pit Bull Terrier

➡ AMERICAN PIT BULL TERRIER

Pit Bull Terriers may be American or British. This American breed weighs up to 80 pounds and is very short, standing 22 inches at most. It comes in all colors and is so variable that it defies "legal" description. The dog was originally bred for fighting in a pit. They are still fought (illegally in most places) and are certainly NOT for the beginner. They are strong and require exercise to keep them fit.

AUSTRALIAN CATTLE DOG ➡

This dog was developed in Australia since the beginning of the 20th century for herding cattle over long distances from range to market. It reaches 45 pounds and stands 20 inches tall at the shoulder.

◀ AMERICAN WATER SPANIEL

This dog originated in the USA in the 20th century. They stand 18 inches tall and weigh up to 45 pounds. Their colors are only solid liver or dark chocolate. Their coats are tightly curled except for a smooth head.

Australian Terrier

AUSTRALIAN SHEPHERD

This dog was developed in the USA. It reaches a height of 23 inches at the shoulder and weighs up to 70 pounds. These are lovely pets. They have moderate coats with dense undercoats. Their basic colors are blue merle, liver merle, black, liver, and red with or without white and/or tan markings.

The 2.5 inch coat is harsh, straight and dense. It appears as a blue/sandy or clear sandy. It makes a nice house pet and can be very active with children.

AUSTRALIAN TERRIER

This dog originated in Australia and is closely related to the Silky Terrier. Both were developed in the 19th century by Australians. This small breed reaches 14 pounds at 10 inches at the shoulder.

Basenji

➥ BASSET HOUND

This dog originated in Britain, having been developed by monks in the Middle Ages. They reach 60 pounds at 14 inches or less. They are disqualified from the show ring if they touch 15 inches! Their coat is short and smooth and any hound color is acceptable. This comical breed has the head and skeleton of a Bloodhound, the color of a Foxhound and the legs of a Dachshund.

◀ BASENJI

This dog was developed in the Congo (now Zaire) as a hunting dog. They reach 24 pounds at about 16 inches at the shoulder. Their tail curls over their back. Their basic colors, with a short, smooth coat, are red, black, or black/tan all with white marks.

▶ The Basset Hound is but one of a group used for hunting rabbits and wounded pheasant and quail. American hunters have trained the Basset Hound to tree opossum, squirrels and raccoons. The popularity of this breed has certainly been enhanced by the use of the breed in many different advertisements.

▶ BEAGLE

This dog was developed in Great Britain as a hound dog. It reaches 30 pounds in weight and reaches 15 inches, though a shorter variety only reaches 13 inches at the shoulder. Their coat is short, smooth and dense and appears in every hound color, usually with a black saddle over brown and white points. These are lovely pets, easily trained and very responsive.

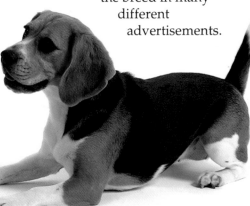

Belgian Shepherd

BEARDED COLLIE

This dog originated in Great Britain. It reaches 60 pounds and stands 22 inches tall at its shoulder. It has a long, harsh, dense coat in black, brown, fawn, or blue with white markings. This dog evolved from the Polish Owczarek Nizinnys which were left in Scotland in the 1500's.

The Bearded Collie was developed by the British dog breeder G. Olive Willison and introduced to the public at the beginning of the war in 1940. This breed carries a rare gene... the *fading gene*. It causes pups like those shown above to lose their intense black color.

BELGIAN SHEPHERD

There are at least four dogs that can claim to be Belgian Shepherds. The one shown here is called the Belgian Tervuren. Tervuren is a city in Belgium. It is a Belgian breed which looks and acts like a German Shepherd but is smaller in build and different in color and coat. This dog weighs 62 pounds and stands 26 inches high. The basic color is a fawn mahogany with a black overlay. They are lovely pets and people who own this dog speak very highly of its intelligence and loyalty.

BEDLINGTON TERRIER

This dog originated in Great Britain in the early 1800s. It reaches 23 pounds at 17.5 inches. The coat is a mixture of hard and soft fur that has a natural curl. It is NOT wiry. It is found in a variety of colors. The breed originated in the mining areas in northern England and was developed from a wirehaired terrier common in that area. They are friendly dogs as a rule.

Bernese Mountain Dog

BERNESE MOUNTAIN DOG ▶

This dog originated in Switzerland and takes its name from the city of Bern. It is a large dog weighing about 88 pounds and standing 27.5 inches at the shoulder. The history of this breed is traceable to the Roman invasion of Switzerland about 2,000 years ago. Though the dog has a very benign temperament which makes it an ideal house pet, it can be seen in Switzerland pulling small carts and herding sheep on rugged mountains.

◀ BICHON FRISE

This dog originated in France and Belgium almost 700 years ago. It is a small dog, reaching a maximum height of 12 inches and is a true companion dog, though categorized as a hunting dog. The long silky coat with a dense undercoat suggests that it can handle the cold weather without much of a problem. The dog is thought to have been brought to France and Belgium by sailors visiting Tenerife, one of the Canary Islands. The tale of how these dogs became popular is very romantic. American soldiers serving in France during the First World War brought back this adorable breed as gifts for their family or loved ones. The dogs became famous little balls of fluff but it took until the 1970s before the dog was recognized the the AKC and the CKC.

BLEU DE GASCOGNE ▶

This is a group of breeds including the Grand Bleu de Gascogne, the Petit Bleu de Gascogne, the Petit Griffon Bleu de Gascogne and the Basset Bleu de Gascogne.

We have chosen the Basset Bleu de Gascogne as our sample of these rare but magnificent breeds. The Basset Bleu was developed in France hundreds of years ago. It looks a lot like a Dachshund, weighing about 40 pounds and reaching 14 inches in height. The coat is short and smooth. It is a hound dog and is found as a tricolor (like the flag of France). The body is mostly white and the tan is only found above the eyes, the cheeks and underside of the ears. The head is black with a few spots. The heavy roaning throughout the white causes the blue appearance.

➤ BORDER COLLIE

This dog originated in Great Britain a long time ago. Its exact history is unknown. It is a medium sized dog weighing about 45 pounds and standing about 20 inches tall at the shoulders. It has a three inch long coat which is thick and straight. It sheds a lot when kept indoors. It comes in many colors, namely, black, blue, chocolate, red, merle in all colors, and markings in tan or white. This is a very friendly dog. It also trains easily. They are such good herders that they even can be trained to herd children who stray from the designated area!

BLOODHOUND ▶

This dog originated in Belgium almost a thousand years ago. It is a large dog which reaches 110 pounds and stands 27 inches tall at the shoulders. It is renowned for its use in law enforcement. The Bloodhound is famous for sniffing a cold train and following it for hours. One Bloodhound followed a trail that was 104 hours old! This same dog tracked down or was a witness against more than 600 criminals. Because of its perseverance, it is NOT an easy dog to train. It wants to do its own thing. Therefore it needs a large, enclosed back yard. I know a farmer who uses Blood-hounds to find his lost calves.

BORDER TERRIER ➤

This dog originated in Great Britain and is a real terrier. It grows to about 12 pounds and a height of 10 inches. Its rough wiry coat makes it an ideal outdoor dog in below-freezing weather without snow...the kind for which central England is known. The usual colors are red to wheaten, grizzle/tan or blue/tan. The dog should not be white except for a small patch on the chest. The name Border Terrier derives from the area between England and Scotland (called the *Border*). The Border Terrier protects sheep from foxes and large vermin that might attack the herd.

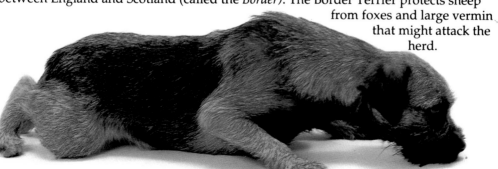

Borzoi

◄ BOSTON TERRIER

This was the first dog my mother bought for me in 1933! It is my mother's favorite breed. Large specimens reach 25 pounds at a height of 17 inches. They have a very short and smooth coat and are found in black and white or brindle and white colors. These dogs were bred down from the pit fighters that were brought to America in the 18th century. Their ancestry contains Pit Bulls, Boxers, English Bull Terriers, French Bulldogs and English Bulldogs. The first breedings took place in 1893. These are friendly, active dogs. They are very intelligent and make great pets. They are not yappy— and they are not classed in the terrier group.

BORZOI ▶

This dog originated in Russia. It is a large dog that grows to 105 pounds and stands 31 inches tall. Their coat is moderately long and silky. It is short on the head. In Russia I have seen them in many colors. The Russian literature records this breed back to the 1600s. Historically, the breed was developed by crossing the Arabian sight hounds with the Russian Tartar coursing hounds. Presently it is known as the Russian Wolfhound and is used for Russian vodka advertisements. Russians are great dog lovers; they pride themselves on exceptional dogs and horses.

BOUVIER DES FLANDRES ▶

This breed originated in Belgium or, perhaps, France, near the Belgian border. This dog weighs about 88 pounds and stands about 27.5 inches high. It has harsh hair which is often described as *like steel wool*. Its colors may be black, fawn, pepper and salt, gray or brindle. It is often referred to as the Belgian Cattle Dog because it is such a great herder. The name *bouvier* comes from the French for *bovine* referring to cows or cattle.

BOXER ▶

This dog originated in Germany and went on to become one of America's favorites. The dog is shown with uncropped ears in the UK but in the USA the dog is usually cropped. Weighing up to 71 pounds, the dog may stand as high as 25 inches. The coat is short and smooth and the colors of the coat are normally fawn or brindle, with or without white points and a white muzzle. The origin of the breed was probably Great Danes and English Bulldogs.

BRIARD ▶

This dog originated in France where it was historically used for herding. The breed weighs up to 75 pounds and reaches 27 inches in height. It has long fur which is slightly wavy and stiff. It occurs in all uniform colors except white, mostly black, fawn, gray or tawny. This is a VERY brave dog and is the official dog of the French army. It has a unique sense of smell and is often used to sniff illegal drugs being carried in sealed containers.

BRITTANY ◀

Often called the *Brittany Spaniel* or the *Epagneul Breton*, this famous gun dog weighs up to 40 pounds and stands 20 inches high. They have a very soft coat which is usually orange/white or liver/white in America, but European dogs may be tri-colored or black/white. Many spaniels came from Spain, but this dog originated in France.

Brussels Griffon

◀ BRUSSELS GRIFFON

Originating in Belgium, the Brussels Griffon is an intelligent, alert and sensitive dog, full of personality. Griffons are small, compact dogs with a short, upturned face. They usually weigh from 6 to 12 pounds and are about 8 inches in height. Their coat can be either rough or smooth. Coat color can be either red, beige, black or black and tan.

BULLDOG ➡

The Bulldog of today is quiet, gentle and affectionate, unlike its early ancestors. Originating in Great Britain, the dog received its name in connection with the sport of bullbaiting, and was used in the sport of dog fighting until 1835. Through careful scientific breeding, it was possible to eliminate the undesirable characteristics and to retain and accentuate the finer qualities of the breed. The Bulldog has a heavy, thick-set body with a short-faced, massive head. They weigh from about 40 to 55 pounds when mature. The skin is soft and loose. The coat is short and close. Coat color is red brindle, other brindles, white, red-fawn and piebald, while black is undesirable.

Bull Terrier

◀ BULLMASTIFF

In 1860, Bullmastiffs were developed by English gamekeepers for protection from poachers. They were created by crossing the English Mastiff with the Bulldog, making a fearless, tough, agile and quiet tracker. Their job was to track, knock down and keep the poacher captive until the gamekeeper arrived. Today, they are docile and alert pets who are protective of children and property making them dependable family pets.

These are large dogs measuring 25 to 27 inches at the withers and weighing from 110 to 130 pounds. The coat is smooth, short and dense with the coloring being red, fawn or brindle, often with a black mask.

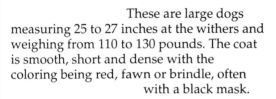

BULL TERRIER ◆

Strong, agile, peaceable and friendly describe the Bull Terrier. This breed was developed in Great Britain around 1835 by crossing the Bulldog with the now extinct white English Terrier, and later with the Spanish Pointer to give it a bit more size. It was used as a fighting dog and was bred by sportsmen with a sense of fair play. It was taught to defend himself and master, but not to instigate hostility. The Bull Terrier is an athlete with a muscular and strongly built body. It has a short, flat coat, that is white, or any color other than white with or without markings. They weigh from 52 to 62 pounds and are about 22 inches in height. The full shaped head gives it a distinctive appearance.

Cairn Terrier

◀ CAIRN TERRIER

This native of Scotland received its name from piles of rocks that served as marks for boundaries or graves. The cairns were hiding places for small mammals such as foxes. Packs of the terriers were kept for hunting and for extermination purposes. The Cairn is an active, curious and cheerful dog. They are well muscled and sturdy and make an ideal companion for a child. The coat of the Cairn is rough and wiry and is any color except white. They weigh 13 to 14 pounds and are about 9½ to 10 inches in height.

CHIHUAHUA ▶

The origin of the Chihuahua is not completely known, but it first became prominent around 1895 in Mexico City. It is the smallest dog, weighing from 1 to 6 pounds. It has either a short and smooth coat or a long and soft coat with feathering on the legs, feet and ears. The coat color is varied and can be solid or marked. The Chihuahua is an alert and playful dog and is often favored by the elderly.

◀ CARDIGAN WELSH CORGI

The Cardigan Welsh Corgi is thought to have been brought to Wales around 1200 BC by migrating Celts from Central Europe. These dogs were used by farmers to drive cattle to pasture, not really herding them, but nipping at their heels to drive them. Because of their short legs, they could duck close to the ground, avoiding dangerous kicks. These low set dogs are long in body with a moderately heavy bone structure and a low set, fox-like tail. Their coat is medium length, harsh and dense. The coat color can be red, sable, black, brindle, tricolor and blue merle. They weigh about 28 to 30 pounds and are around 12 inches in height. These dogs are affectionate, loyal, obedient and even-tempered.

CHESAPEAKE BAY RETRIEVER ▶

There is no real accurate history of the origin of this breed. It was developed in the USA most likely from English stock. This dog is a hard and willing worker with a mental and physical toughness that made it famous for its retrieving abilities in the rough, icy, saltwater Bay of the Chesapeake. The coat is short, thick and coarse with a fine woolly undercoat. It is almost oily and sheds water like that of a duck's feathers and insulates the dog from the wet and cold. Coat color will vary from a dark brown to dead grass color, which was preferred, to provide camouflage. Males will weigh from 65 to 80 pounds and range from 23 to 26 inches in height, while females may run 10 pounds lighter and about 2 inches smaller. They are devoted family dogs that need sufficient exercise and thrive on having a job to do to keep them happy.

◀ CAVALIER KING CHARLES SPANIEL

This breed has its origins in Great Britain. They weigh from 10 to 18 pounds and are 12 to 13 inches in height. Their coat is long and silky with feathering on the legs, chest and ears. Coat color is either solid red, red and white, black and tan or tricolor. They make gentle, affectionate companions.

CHINESE CRESTED ▶

These dogs have their origin in both Africa and China. They evolved in Africa from the African hairless and through breeding were reduced in size by the Chinese. There are two types of the Chinese Crested, the Hairless and the Powderpuff. The Hairless has hair only on the head, feet and tail, while the Powderpuff is fully coated. The hair on both is soft and silky and comes in any color or color combination. They weigh from 5 to 10 pounds and are about 11 to 13 inches in height. Loving, playful and entertaining describe the Chinese Crested.

Chow Chow

CURLY-COATED RETRIEVER ▶

Developed in Great Britain, this retriever is at home in the water. Its coat is short and close with crisp curls, except on the face which is smooth. The coat repels water and is very quick drying. Coat color is either black or liver. This breed weighs about 70 to 80 pounds and is 25 to 27 inches in height at the withers. Intelligent, sweet tempered and easily trainable describe this breed, as well as being independent, fearless and protective.

◄ COCKER SPANIEL

Also known as the American Cocker Spaniel, this dog is smaller than the English Cocker Spaniel. It is one of the most popular breeds today, no wonder, with its happy and affectionate disposition. It is also an energetic, playful and intelligent breed that is easily trained. This breed was developed in the USA and was a valued gun dog, thus labeled the smallest member of the sporting-dog family. The coat of the Cocker is long and silky with abundant feathering. Coat color is black, black and tan, chocolate, red, buff, sable, cream and particolored. It weighs from 24 to 28 pounds and is 14 to 15 inches in height.

COLLIE ◄

There are two varieties of Collie, the Rough Collie, having a long and dense coat and the Smooth Collie, having a short smooth coat. Both types weigh from 50 to 75 pounds and are 22 to 26 inches in height. Coat color can be sable and white, blue merle, tricolor or white. They were herding dogs that were developed in Great Britain. Collies are extremely loyal family companions and are also very docile and gentle, making them an excellent choice for a child's pet.

Curly-Coated Retriever

CHOW CHOW ▾

Originating in China, the earliest traces of this breed were from the 11th century BC. They served many functions in China such as guard dogs, hunting dogs, flock and draft dogs and were also used as food, with their coat being made into clothing. They were first brought to the Western World in the 1800s. Chows are muscular and sturdy dogs with heavy bone structure. Coat color can be red, black, blue, cinnamon or cream. The coat can be one of two types, either Rough, which is long and straight forming ruffs around the head and neck, or Smooth, which is shorter and dense. Both have a soft, thick undercoat. Unique to the Chow breed is the black color of the tongue, lips and gums.

This breed is intelligent with an independent nature and makes an excellent guard dog. It is extremely loyal to its family, while being aloof with strangers.

Dachshund

DACHSHUND

The Dachshund originated in Germany and was developed for hunting purposes. They are bred in two sizes, Miniature and Standard, and come in three coat varieties, Longhaired, Smooth and Wirehaired. Each was developed for different hunting needs. Coat color can be red, cream or two-color, with tan being combined with black, chocolate, gray and fawn and also a doppled pattern. The Miniatures weigh less than 9 pounds while the Standards are from 15 to 25 pounds. The Dachshund is full of energy and very playful with no display of shyness.

DALMATIAN ▶

The origin of the Dalmatian is not known, but early records note the breed as being first found in the region of Dalmatia. Throughout history, it seems that this dog has held almost every job: hunter, dog of war, shepherd, circus and carriage dog, but he is most noted as the "Firehouse Dog." Everyone can *spot* a Dalmatian due to its unique coat pattern of white with black or liver-colored spots distributed over the entire body. It weighs from 50 to 55 pounds and is 19 to 23 inches in height. A good amount of exercise is needed for this dog. It has an outgoing personality and an even temper and makes a good watchdog.

Doberman Pinscher

DANDIE DINMONT TERRIER ▸

First recorded in the 1700s, this breed originated in the Cheviot Hills, which lie between England and Scotland, and was developed for hunting badger and otter. The body is long and low to the ground, being 8 to 11 inches in height; the dog weighs 18 to 24 pounds. The coat has a mixture of both harsh (not wiry) and soft hair, in either a pepper or mustard color. The loving and intelligent Dandie Dinmont makes a great family companion.

DOBERMAN PINSCHER ◂

Originating in Germany, the Doberman was created to be the perfect guardian. There were many different breeds used to get the required result, but it took a relatively short time for the type to be established. The Doberman is a solid dog with good muscle and power, having both speed and endurance. The coat is smooth and short, color being black, red, blue or fawn, with tan markings.

Being of medium size, it weighs from 66 to 88 pounds and is 24 to 28 inches in height. It is a loyal and obedient dog, full of energy. It is also fearless and very alert, making it one of the best watch or guard dog breeds.

English Foxhound

◀ ENGLISH FOXHOUND

Fox hunting in England during the 13th century required a specific hound for trailing the wily red fox. Bicolor or tricolor with white predominating, this hound stands 23 to 27 inches in height and can weigh anywhere between 55 to 70 pounds. A very short, hard coat enables them to follow their foxy friend into many tight places. The basis for the English Foxhound formed from the blood of St. Hubert/Bloodhound type to crosses with faster, lighter hounds, and even to Greyhounds to increase speed.

ENGLISH SPRINGER SPANIEL ➤

In 1902 the Springer was declared its own breed. The leggiest of all spaniels, he stands 19 to 20 inches and weighs 49 to 55 pounds. His coat is close with feathering on the ears, chest, legs and belly. The color can be black or liver with white markings or tricolor. The English Springer Spaniel is the largest of all spaniels and is best known for its ability to "spring" into the bushes and flush out game. His pleasant personality and good looks make for a fine house dog.

◀ ENGLISH SETTER

More than 400 years ago the English Setter was a trained bird dog in England. Setters come in a variety of colors: tricolor, black/white, blue, lemon, orange and liver belton, lemon/white, liver/white, orange/white, and all white. The English Setter usually stands about 24 to 25 inches, and can weigh anywhere from 40 to 70 pounds. Best known for its hunting ability, the name "setter" derives from the old style of hunting, creeping cat-like toward a bird and then sinking slowly between the shoulder blades as they point.

Flat-Coated Retriever

FLAT-COATED RETRIEVER ➤

During the latter half of the 19th century in Great Britain, the Flat-Coated Retriever appeared and attracted immediate attention. The coat is a dense, fine texture of medium length, usually solid black or liver in color, and is easy to care for. Standing 22 to 23 inches tall, this sturdy companion normally weighs between 60 and 70 pounds. The Flat-Coat is a fine land and water retriever with natural talent in marking, retrieving and delivering. The superior qualities of agility, trainability and willingness to please make this not only dog a welcome household pet but a top competitor as well.

◀ ENGLISH TOY SPANIEL

The charming personality of a spaniel in a tiny package of only 10 inches in height and a weight of 9 to 12 pounds, this dog was a valued pet in 16th-century England. Their coat is long, wavy, and silky. Colors include tricolor, solid red, red/white, and black/tan. Tails are docked as with spaniels, and carried level with the back. Protruding eyes and hanging ears must be kept scrupulously clean, but otherwise care is minimal.

FINNISH SPITZ ➤

Native to Finland, this courageous hunting dog is built square and stands 15 to 20 inches tall with a lightness of 25 to 30 pounds for precise hunting. His soft, moderately short, dense coat is normally a chestnut red to pale red-gold in color. Once used for tracking bear and elk, its nickname, "the barking dog," was attributed to him for his unique method of hunting. His lively manner, along with use of keen senses directs him to a treed game bird. Then with a melodious type bark, almost hypnotic, the hunter is given a chance to move in.

FIELD SPANIEL ➤

Originating in England during the mid-1800s, this breed of medium-sized spaniel was not perfected until the mid-1900s. Usually liver or black in color, with a height averaging 18 inches, and weighing 35 to 50 pounds, the Field Spaniel has become a useful and handsome breed. At one time, trends of fashion nearly ruined this noble, upstanding sporting dog by purposely breeding a grotesque creature with very short, crooked legs, and an elongated, weak body.

Fox Terrier

GIANT SCHNAUZER

Originating in Germany for sheep and cattle herders, the Giant Schnauzer is the largest of the Schnauzer family. This robust dog usually weighs between 70 to 77 pounds, and stands 23 to 27 inches at the withers. His coat is hard, wiry and very dense, usually solid black or salt and pepper in color. It has become known as one of the most useful, powerful and enduring of the working breeds.

FRENCH BULLDOG

The toy bulldogs were developed in England, but it was the French who perfected the breed in the mid-19th century. They have a moderately fine, short, smooth coat usually brindle, fawn, piebald or white in color. Weighing 22 to 28 pounds and standing approximately 12 inches, they are popular as an indoor pet. The bat ear and skull shape are two of the distinguishing features of the French Bulldog.

GOLDEN RETRIEVER

This breed was developed in Great Britain by hunters who wanted a versatile retriever and upland game hunter. A dense, water repellent coat, usually soft, pale moon to a lustrous gold, lies flat to the body and requires routine brushing. The Retriever stands 21 to 25 inches in height and weighs 65 to 70 pounds. This loving, easygoing companion needs sufficient exercise to avoid excess poundage.

FOX TERRIER

Ancient breed of English origin, the Fox Terrier is one of the best known pure-bred dogs. In 1985 the distinction between the Smooth and the Wire Fox Terrier became effective. Both stand between 13 to 15 inches tall and weigh approximately 17 pounds. Coat color is mostly white, with liver, brindle or red markings. They are alert with boundless amounts of energy.

GERMAN SHEPHERD DOG

The German Shepherd originated in late 1800s from sheep-herding dogs in Germany. This strong, well-muscled animal stands 24 to 26 inches in height and has a body weight averaging 75 to 95 pounds. The double coat is moderately short, straight and lies close to the body. Color is either black/tan, sable, or all black. For generations the German Shepherd has been considered man's servant and companion. They have a natural aptitude for learning and a keen sense of smell, along with qualities such as courage and intelligence.

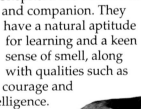

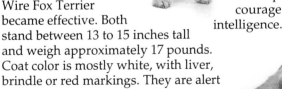

◀ GERMAN SHORTHAIRED POINTER

German breeders of early 1800s created this versatile gun dog. Weighing 55 to 70 pounds and standing 23 to 25 inches tall, the German Shorthaired Pointer gave the German and Austrian sportsmen a smaller, faster breed, with a superb sense of smell. The most common color is liver roan. Other colors are liver, liver and white, and liver and white spotted and ticked. An aristocratic, well balanced, powerful and agile breed, the German Shorthaired Pointer is a wonderful house and watchdog.

GREAT DANE ▶

Originating in Germany, Great Danes served as boar hunters and protectors. These well-balanced, powerful creatures are no less than 30 inches at shoulder length and exceed 100 pounds. They are bred in a variety of colors, such as brindle, fawn, blue, black and harlequin. A short, thick, smooth and glossy coat adds to the beauty of the smoothly muscled body. The Great Dane is well balanced for his size and has a combination of dignity, strength and elegance.

◀ GREAT PYRENEES

This dog originated in the Pyrenees Mountains that separate France from Spain. It is an enormous and powerful dog. Coat color is white, weight is from 90 to 140 pounds and height is about 32 inches. It is a docile, easygoing breed that is extremely patient with children.

GERMAN WIREHAIRED POINTER ▼

Developed in Germany, this dog was bred to be multi-talented. Among its skills are speed, scenting, pointing, retrieving and trailing. Other traits include the liking of water, ease of training and intelligence. It is an active breed requiring plenty of exercise. Coat color is solid liver or a combination of liver and white. Height is between 24 to 26 inches and weight is from about 60 to 70 pounds.

◀ GREYHOUND

Greyhounds were developed in Great Britain and were in great demand by English nobility. Weighing 60 to 70 pounds and standing 27 to 30 inches, this sleek, muscled and speedy breed has been known to reach speeds of 45mph. Its coat is short, smooth and can be of any color. Modern Greyhounds make gentle, well-behaved pets and are enjoyed by thousands on racetracks all over the United States.

Ibizan Hound

◀ IBIZAN HOUND

The Ibizan Hound can be traced back as far as 3400 BC in Egypt, where many artifacts were discovered in Pharaohs' tombs depicting the breed. This breed was brought to the Balearic Islands located off the coast of Spain by trading ships. It received its name from one of these islands called Ibiza and was used as a hunting dog.

The coat can be either shorthaired or wirehaired and is solid white, red or a combination. The height of the dog is between 22½ and 27½ inches, weighing from 42 to 55 pounds. It is a slender but strong breed, being very agile and fast. An excellent family pet, it is loyal, affectionate and even tempered.

IRISH TERRIER ◆

Originating in Ireland, it is believed to be one of the oldest of the terrier breeds and was first recorded in 1875. This breed is a true guardsman and very loyal, as well as a great playmate, spirited and even tempered. The coat is dense and wiry, being colored red, golden red, red wheaten or wheaten. The height of this dog is about 18 inches at the shoulder and weight is from 25 to 27 pounds.

◀ ICELAND DOG

This breed is from Iceland. Its ancestors are thought to have been brought there by Vikings in 880 AD. It is a herding breed with no hunting instincts. The coat is thick and coarse with the color being a dirty white, wheaten, sable or black, usually with white markings. The Iceland Dog weighs about 20 to 30 pounds and is 12 to 16 inches in height. This is a very active, affectionate and alert breed.

IRISH SETTER ▶

Native to Ireland, the Irish Setter first came into popular notice early in the 18th century. The breed was originally known as the Irish Red Setter because of its mahogany or rich colored coat. Standing over two feet tall at the shoulder, the dog has a straight, fine, glossy coat that is longer on the ears, tail, chest and back of legs, and it weighs about 70 pounds. The Irish Setter is bold and at the same time is gentle as well as lovable and loyal.

Jack Russell Terrier

IRISH WATER SPANIEL ▶

Appearing in Ireland in the 1830s, this dog was used to hunt water fowl, being a strong swimmer and noted retriever. This breed stands 21 to 24 inches in height at the withers and weighs from 45 to 65 pounds. It has only one coat color, liver, which is curly and tight on the body, neck and top of tail and loose over the rest of the body, except for the face which is smooth. This playful and trainable breed makes a good family pet.

ITALIAN GREYHOUND ◆

Developed in Italy, this dog was bred specifically as a lap dog. It is definitely not a breed to be kept outside, but a house dog, being a quiet, clean breed that is easily cared for. There are 2 varieties, one weighing up to 8 pounds and the other weighing over that. They are 13 to 15 inches in height with a short and smooth coat being colored white, cream, fawn, red, mouse and blue.

◆ JACK RUSSELL TERRIER

Originating in Great Britain, this breed was developed as a fox hunter by the Rev. Jack Russell in the mid 1800s. It weighs 12 to 18 pounds and comes in two sizes, one measuring 9 to 12 inches, the other 12 to 15 inches. Coat texture can be either smooth or rough and color is white over 50% of its body, marked with black, brown or both. Color was important so that the hunter could tell the difference between fox and dog. They were also used as ratters. Affectionate and sweet, they make great children's pets and require plenty of exercise.

◆ IRISH WOLFHOUND

A native of Ireland, the Irish Wolfhound is the largest and tallest of the hounds being 32 to 34 inches in height at the shoulder and weighing from 105 to over 120 pounds. The coat is rough and hard and is black, gray, brindle, red, fawn or white in color. Throughout history this dog is known for its great hunting ability, speed and unmatchable power. This breed is also known for its gentle, calm nature, making it an ideal human companion. Its need for exercise is great.

Japanese Chin

JAPANESE CHIN ▶

The Japanese Chin originated in Japan. The breed exists in two varieties: the smaller variety must weigh under 7 pounds while the larger variety must weigh under the 7 pound limit. The small area in which most Japanese live has made them a people of miniatures. Thus the Chin is bred for small size...the smaller the better. Its silky, soft coat is found in black/white or red/white, in all shades.

JAPANESE SPITZ ▼

This dog originated in Japan where it reaches 13 pounds at 16 inches. The Japanese prefer a smaller size. This is a lovely dog with thick white fur. The dog descended from Scandinavian breeds. They look a great deal like the spitz breeds of Germany.

◀ KEESHOND

This dog originated in Holland. It is a mid-sized dog reaching about 55 pounds at 17 inches. It has long, thick fur which has the color of a wolf. It is sometimes called the *Wolfspitz.* These dogs are part of the legend of a Viking invasion where the Viking ship was wrecked and the only survivors were these dogs.

▲ KOMONDOR

This breed originated in Hungary where it grows to 150 pounds. This dog is bred for size...the bigger the better! It generally reaches about 2 feet in height. This is a 1,000-year-old breed which is a herder and protector. It protects sheep, cattle, children and property. Its huge size and odd appearance frighten wrong-doers.

◀ KERRY BLUE TERRIER

This dog originated in Ireland where it grows to 40 pounds and stands almost 20 inches high. It has a lovely soft, thick coat of wavy black fur. This terrier has the personality of a typical Irishman...lively, intelligent and friendly. This terrier takes care of the flock and attacks small animals that threaten their charges. Many reports of them chasing otters into the deep water to kill them have been verified. Kerry Blues are born black but gradually turn blue.

LABRADOR RETRIEVER ◗

This popular breed originated in Great Britain where it reaches 75 pounds at 2 feet in height. The coat is solid black, chocolate or yellow and is thick, dense and with an insulating undercoat which makes it practically waterproof. The dogs are very much favorites because they are gentle, loyal and extremely intelligent. Many are used to assist the handicapped. One author describes the personality of these dogs as willing to please. Of course they are used for bird hunting where they retrieve ducks which are shot down over water.

◖ LAKELAND TERRIER

This dog originated in Great Britain where it reaches a mere 17 pounds at 15 inches in height. It has a hard, wiry coat in blue, black, liver, black/tan, blue/tan, red, red grizzle, grizzle/tan and wheaten. These are fox hunters which were trained to go into the fox's tunnel and kill it, hopefully bringing the body out for the hunters to see.

KUVASZ ◆

This dog originated in Hungary. It is a large dog which easily reaches over 100 pounds at over 2 feet in height. Its white (or ivory) coat is wavy and not too long. It does shed if kept indoors. Hungarian kings used Kuvaszok for hunting and personal protection. This is a powerful, loyal dog but may be a danger to strangers...especially strange animals. These are great companion dogs and are extremely protective of their friends, whether they be sheep or children. They need constant brushing if their coat is to be kept tangle-free.

LHASA APSO ◆

This dog originated in Tibet where it reaches about 11 inches. It has a heavy, straight, hard and dense coat which usually is golden, sandy or honey in color, but it exists in many other colors, even parti-colors like black/white. These dogs have a history of almost 3,000 years and were given by the Tibetans to guests and friends as good luck charms. These lap dogs require a lot of grooming.

Maltese

MANCHESTER TERRIER →

This breed originated in Great Britain, probably in the area of Manchester. Two varieties are known: the Toy Manchester Terrier is a smallish dog which reaches about 12 pounds. The Manchester Terrier is larger and, again, has two categories: the smaller one reaches 16 pounds and the larger varieties ranges from 16 to 22 pounds. Otherwise they are all identical in color, coat and behavior. Their coat, by the way, is easy to care for as it is short and smooth.

MALTESE ←

This tiny lapdog originated in Italy where they are supposed to weigh in under 7 pounds. The smaller the better. The preferred color is pure white though slightly darker ears are allowed but not preferred. This long, flat, silky fur must be groomed constantly as the tangles are difficult to remove. The Maltese is a thousand-year-old breed and takes its name from the Island of Malta off the coast of Italy. Tiny specimens are highly prized and very expensive. In spite of its size, the dog is very playful and hardy.

MASTIFF ←

This huge dog originated in Great Britain. It can weigh almost 200 pounds and stand up to 30 inches in height at the shoulder. Its short, smooth coat comes in apricot, fawn, or fawn/brindle, all with a black muzzle. Some older books refer to this breed as *Old English Mastiff*. These dogs, originally used as guard dogs, are now great companion dogs with a loyal dedication. They rarely can be sold as adults because they do not re-adapt to new people.

MINIATURE PINSCHER ▶

Looking like the Doberman Pinscher, this tiny dog barely reaches 10 pounds and a foot in height. Its short smooth coat is usually seen in black/tan, chocolate/tan or stag red. Its ears are usually cropped and its tail docked. These are fun loving, bouncy dogs which get along well with children. Some strains befriend only one member of the family, usually the first person to imprint on him. My wife brought our MinPin home from the breeder and the dog associated with only her ever since.

▲ MINIATURE BULL TERRIER

This breed originated in Britain where it reaches from 10 to 40 pounds and stands 10 to 14 inches in height. It has a short, harsh coat and is found in solid white with head markings of brindle, red, fawn, black/tan, black brindle or solid colors with white markings. These were used as successful ratters which worked well with their larger brethren. The dog is hardy and well behaved when trained properly.

Most Manchester owners infrequently groom their dog's coat unless they are being shown or have become soiled with dirt. This dog was used for ratting and rabbit coursing in Manchester.

Miniature Schnauzer

NEWFOUNDLAND ▶

This dog originated in Canada where it can reach 150 pounds! Its height often exceeds 27 inches. It has medium-long fur which is very dense and thick and runs in black, bronze or parti-color. They were used basically for life-saving work bringing rope cables to sinking boats and rescuing drowning seamen from rough seas. This is a noble breed which has proven its worth for many years.

▲ MINIATURE SCHNAUZER

This dog was developed in Germany. Actually there are three Schnauzers: the Miniature, the Standard, and the Giant. The Miniature reaches 15 pounds and stands 14 inches tall at the shoulder. The Standard goes to 33 pounds and 20 inches at the shoulder. Their hair is wiry and rough and is colored salt and pepper, black or black/tan. Schnauzers are used in Germany for such farm tasks as ratting, herding and guarding both people and property.

NORWEGIAN ELKHOUND ➤

There are two Norwegian Elkhounds originating in Norway. One variety is gray, wolf-like. The other variety is solid black. The gray Norwegian Elkhound stands about 20 inches tall and weighs in at 20 kilograms or 44 pounds. It has a short, stiff (coarse) and thick fur with a heavy doubling that makes it especially suitable for cold climates. This is one of the world's oldest breeds dating back to the Stone Age. In Norway they are used for hunting elk, lynx, bear, moose and wolf. They make great watchdogs and hunting companions.

◀ NORWICH TERRIER

This dog originated in Britain where it barely reaches 12 pounds at 10 inches of height. It has a wiry, hard coat that stays close to the body. It is not difficult to groom this dog. Its basic colors are from red to wheaten. These terriers were used with foxhounds to go after prey that went into small holes. Today the breed is a friendly family dog that is growing in popularity. Like most other terriers, they are active, a bit yappy, and slightly independent.

◀ OLD ENGLISH SHEEPDOG

This dog originated in Great Britain where it weighs in at 66 pounds and stands at least 22 inches. Because of their very long, profuse and shaggy coat they actually look larger and heavier than they really are. Obvious from the name, this is a herding breed. As puppies these are marvelously beautiful, friendly and irresistible. But when reality sets in, you have a mature dog that requires constant grooming and infinite patience in training. The dog is a good family dog and is protective of children when it gets to know them very well.

PAPILLON

The proper name for the Papillon is Continental Toy Spaniel Papillon. The Papillon originated in France/Belgium and must stay under 12 inches in height. It has a magnificent coat which is long, fine and silky. The dog is basically white, but it must have a special mask which covers both eyes and ears. This coloration is the basis for the name *papillon* which means *butterfly* in French. Despite their coat being long and silky, it is easy to care for.

OTTERHOUND ➡

This breed originated in Great Britain where it grows to a huge size...120 pounds at 27 inches of height. It has a coat which is medium length, hard and wiry, waterproof because of the heavy oily exudate and a substantial undercoat. This dog is ready for any kind of weather. Its basic colors are grizzle or wheaten, black/tan, liver/tan and tricolor. Like other hounds, they are warm, affectionate dogs, very loyal to their masters.

◀ PEKINGESE

This breed originated in China where it is divided into three categories. The most valuable category are the dogs under 6 pounds. Then comes the middle class of 6 to 8 pounds, followed by the heavyweights of 8 to 14 pounds. Their coat is long, straight, harsh and profuse. They have a heavy undercoat and require daily grooming. These are true lap dogs and they prefer humans to other dogs as companions. They come in many colors; as a matter of fact, all colors are acceptable for most show purposes. The dogs became famous in England when one was given to Queen Victoria.

◀ POODLE

The breed originated in France and is recognized in three sizes. The Toy Poodle is under 10 inches; the Miniature Poodle is between 10-15 inches; the Standard Poodle is over 15 inches. They occur in every solid color; parti-colors are rejected from showing. Though the Poodle was initially trained as a gun dog, it has been so inbred for show purposes that they have lost most if not all of their hunting abilities.

PODENGO CANARIO ▶

If you ever wanted a very rare dog breed this is it. These 40 pound dogs stand about 2 feet high. They were developed in the Canary Islands which belong to Spain. No kennel club recognizes the breed as yet. It appears in a shorthair or wirehair variety.

◀ POMERANIAN

This dog originated in Pomerania, Germany. It was brought to England by Queen Victoria in 1888 and quickly became a favorite lap dog. Reaching a mere 3 to 7 pounds and less than a foot tall, this lovely breed sports a long, soft coat in as many as 12 colors! Weekly grooming is necessary.

◀ POINTER

This lovely dog was developed in Britain. It may reach 66 pounds at a height of 2 feet at the shoulder. It occurs in a short, dense and smooth coat which is colored liver, lemon, black or orange, with or without white. These are wonderful companion and hunting dogs; they are excellent gun dogs and are used extensively worldwide for this purpose.

PEMBROKE WELSH CORGI ☙

There are two Welsh Corgis, the Cardigan and the Pembroke. The Pembroke reaches 28 pounds at 12 inches. It has a medium-short coat which is harsh and dense. It occurs in red, sable, fawn, black/tan and may have white markings on their legs, chest and neck. These are herders which were used extensively in Wales. They are hardy and were always outside with the herd. Queen Elizabeth II, the reigning Queen of England, keeps this breed, thus making it the fashionable dog to have. They are excellent pets which have been known since 1200 AD.

❧ Poodle puppies are irresistible to the author. I have had Poodles for over 40 years. My silver Miniature Poodle was bred to another silver Mini...she produced livers with liver noses! Having discussed this with several dog geneticists, we concluded that silver is a dominant color in Poodles and that recessive genes for liver color must have existed in both parents of the liver-colored puppies.

Portuguese Water Dog

◀ PORTUGUESE WATER DOG

This dog originated in Portugal where it reaches from 35 to 55 pounds and grows from 16 to 22 inches in height. It has a lovely, shiny coat which is wavy and curled. Its basic colors are white, black or liver with varying degrees of white markings. This is a wonderful pet which can be used for protection, hunting, or companionship.

◀ PULI

This Hungarian breed reaches 40 pounds when it is 20 inches in height. It is famous for its thick, curly coat which is very coarse and develops cords. Its coat acts as an insulation against the cold as it guards herds of cattle. It also serves to protect the body from the frequent kicks it receives from the cows. It is found in all solid colors. They develop the thick, curly coat very early in their lives. The grooming of these dogs is burdensome. Some people groom them in Afro styles, but for showing they must be corded.

◀ PUG

The Pug originated in China where it may reach 18 pounds at 11 inches in height. It has a short, smooth coat which appears in apricot, silver-fawn, or black. The mask must be black. This is really a miniature mastiff which has become a lapdog. Because it can be lazy, it easily gains weight and its diet must be closely regulated. The dog has been in Europe since 1533.

Rottweiler

◀ RHODESIAN RIDGEBACK

This breed originated in South Africa where it may reach 100 pounds in exceptional cases and stand 30 inches high. The standards of showing require a maximum of 75 pounds at 27 inches. Their coats are short and glossy with colors of wheaten red. White markings are rare but acceptable. These are active dogs with a mind of their own so they must be firmly trained as puppies.

Undisciplined dogs of any breed are a nuisance, but Rhodesians are intolerable. They get their name from the ridge of hair growing on the top of their backs.

◀ ROTTWEILER

This German breed is currently one of the world's most popular dogs. It reaches a weight of 110 pounds at 27 inches and has a short, smooth coat. It only occurs in black and tan. Their main use was as herders and guard dogs. When herders slept, they would tie their money belts around their Rottweilers' necks.

Today, Rottweilers are still being used as guard dogs. They are massive and tough enough to intimidate most burglars.

The Rottweiler's tail is docked to a small stub. It has small drop ears and is a lovable pet, but usually loyal to one person as many dogs are.

Saint Bernard

SAINT BERNARD ☙

This dog originated in Switzerland where it grows to an immense size. Many specimens reach over 200 pounds and measure over 30 inches at the shoulder. They come in two coat varieties: a short and smooth, or a medium long. In all cases the coat is red with lots of white. This is a true mastiff.

Saint Bernard

▶ This Saint Bernard puppy is very young and is but a fraction of its adult size. His dark red markings against a solid white body are perfectly acceptable for show purposes. Purchasing a show-quality Saint Bernard puppy can be hopefully quite reasonable.

In the 900s, almost 1100 years ago, a monk named Bernard of Menthon was canonized Saint Bernard. He lived high in the Swiss Alps and dedicated his life to rescuing people trapped in the snow and frequent snow slides. He used a large, strong dog which eventually became known as the Saint Bernard. These wonderful dogs grow as large as 305 pounds, which is the record. They are so strong that one of them pulled a cart weighing 6400 pounds a distance of 15 feet in 90 seconds!

They also are great puppy producers. The record for puppies was awarded to a Saint Bernard named *Careless Ann*...she had 23 puppies!

As a giant breed they have all the problems associated with other huge dogs. They walk in a lumbering fashion, they slobber and are expensive to feed. Their excrement is also something to deal with, so be sure you can handle the problems before you buy one of these gorgeous puppies.

Saluki

SAMOYED ▶

These lovely white or cream dogs were bred in Siberia many years ago by the Eskimos. They were used for everything including herding, sled pulling and guarding.

They were always friendly dogs because the Eskimos would sleep with them to stay warm. Their coat is very long and stands off the body. There is a thick undercoat. Experts say those Samoyeds which are used for herding are not used for sledding and vice versa.

◀ SCHIPPERKE

This dog originated in Belgium. It reaches a maximum of 18 inches and has a very special fur. The coat is abundant, harsh, straight yet attractive. American breeders prefer a solid black dog, but some breeders go for other attractive solid colors. The tail of the Schipperke is completely removed, probably due to a legend. These dogs were popular with shoemakers because rats were a constant problem since they attacked and ate the leather. The dogs also ate the leather and finally one shoemaker became so angry at a neighbor's Schipperke that he cut off its tail. This made the dog look attractive and the fad stayed with the breed!

◀ SALUKI

The Saluki originated in Iran where they have been raised for thousands of years. They grow to about 28 inches and are slender and racy. They are soft coated with a silky fur that has a lot of feathering. There are some varieties, though, that are devoid of feathering. Often referred to as the Persian Greyhound, these dogs appear in white, cream, fawn, gold, red, grizzle/tan, tricolor or black and tan. They have been documented as far back as 3600 BC and are still kept as honored pets under the Persian name *El Hor*, the noble one!

SCOTTISH DEERHOUND ⬧

This breed originated in Britain hundreds of years ago. It reaches a weight of 110 pounds when it is 32 inches high. It has a harsh coat which means it does well outdoors and in the woods. Breeders are aiming for a softer, but not woollier, coat. The color varies from dark gray to blue gray or brindles, yellows, reds and a red fawn. They have black ears and mask. White is allowed on the breast and toes but dogs without white are more desirable. These make pets for people who have lots of room and patience to train the dog properly.

⬧ SCOTTISH TERRIER

This dog was perfected in Great Britain where it achieves a size of 11 inches and a weight of about 23 pounds. It has a wiry coat and occurs in black, brindle wheaten, gray or grizzled, but NOT white, as some ads for whiskey indicate by showing a black and white Scotty. President Franklin Delano Roosevelt made the breed famous in America with his Scottie he called *Fala*. The breed became a respectable member of the dog world in 1859 when it began to appear at dog shows as a pure breed. These dogs are very strong-willed and require thorough discipline training when they are young. If you haven't the time for the puppy, don't buy one.

SEALYHAM TERRIER ⬤

This breed originated in Great Britain where it reaches 25 pounds at 11 inches. It came from Wales and only arrived in America in the mid-1950s. It has a wiry coat with a thick undercoat. It requires a lot of grooming if it is to be kept in its formal condition. These are very game animals and like hunting for small game especially rats, rabbits, squirrels and ferrets. These highly specialized dogs are usually owned by exceptional people who have the means and time to devote to this breed.

Shar-Pei

◀ ➤ SHAR-PEI

This breed originated in China. The Chinese seem to have a passion for breeding monsters. Their famous goldfish breeds with popping eyes (called *telescopes*) or eyes pointing up to heaven (celestial goldfish) are just two of a dozen weird goldfish. They have the same passion for dogs.

What the Shar-Pei lacks in looks, it makes up in love. They may grow large, up to 55 pounds at 20 inches height. Their coat may be fawn, cream, red, black or chocolate and their fur is short and bristly without an undercoat. They love people and must always be with them or they do not thrive.

This is a fighting dog and the theory is that when they are grabbed on the skin by an opponent, they can still turn and bite the enemy.

Shetland Sheepdog

SHETLAND SHEEPDOG

The two puppies shown here demonstrate how nice they are. These are wonderful pets and if you have the chance to own them, take it. But understand that they have long fur and they must be groomed to look well. The Sheltie is a high-energy dog, ideal for both apartment and country life. He is biddable and happily adapts to his owner's lifestyle.

The Shetland Sheepdog originated in Great Britain. It reaches 16 inches in height and has long, dense and harsh coat which appears in black, blue merle or sable, marked with white and/or tan. These are highly intelligent dogs, originally used for herding, but easily trained to compete in obedience trials where they do very well.

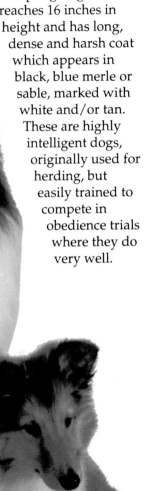

Shiba Inu

SHIBA INU ▶

The Japanese word for *dog* is *inu*. This dog originated in Japan and has the typical tightly curled tail of most other Oriental dogs. It reaches a weight of 30 pounds at a height of 15 inches. It has a double coat which is very dense and harsh. It appears in red (the Japanese preference), black/tan, black sesame, and perhaps very light red. The Shiba is clean and independent and makes a delightful, if somewhat demanding, pet.

◀ SHIH TZU

This breed originated in Tibet and reaches a maximum of 19 pounds. It almost reaches a foot in height and has a long, dense coat which is not too harsh. It appears in all dog colors. The Japanese sometimes refer to this dog as the Chrysanthemum Dog, and use it for herding. Choose your Shih Tzu with great care and be aware of eye problems in the puppy's parents.

SIBERIAN HUSKY ▶

This breed was an ancient dog, millions of years old. It was used in the Stone Age,too. Probably it was on Earth before people! It grows to 60 pounds at 2 feet in height and was perfected in the USA. It has a thick coat with a heavy undercoat to protect it from the cold. It looks like a wolf and its eyes are frightening to some people. They are easily mistaken for wolves and are active dogs that need active masters. They are used for sled pulling, hunting, herding and guard duty. They are very loyal and friendly. They thrive in the cold and lose a lot of hair if kept in a warm house all year.

Siberian Husky

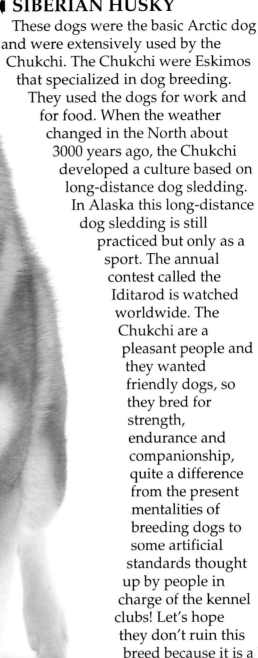

◀ SIBERIAN HUSKY

These dogs were the basic Arctic dog and were extensively used by the Chukchi. The Chukchi were Eskimos that specialized in dog breeding. They used the dogs for work and for food. When the weather changed in the North about 3000 years ago, the Chukchi developed a culture based on long-distance dog sledding. In Alaska this long-distance dog sledding is still practiced but only as a sport. The annual contest called the Iditarod is watched worldwide. The Chukchi are a pleasant people and they wanted friendly dogs, so they bred for strength, endurance and companionship, quite a difference from the present mentalities of breeding dogs to some artificial standards thought up by people in charge of the kennel clubs! Let's hope they don't ruin this breed because it is a wonderful pet dog.

Silky Terrier

SILKY TERRIER ▶

This miniature terrier originated in Australia. It may be as heavy as 10 pounds and reach a height of 9 inches. It has a phenomenal coat which is 5-6 inches long and is flat, very fine and silky and extremely glossy. Its color is called *blue/tan*. This breed is about 150 years old and is the ideal lap dog. Constant grooming is a must if the dog is not to degenerate into ugly tangles and knots. Some breeders prefer the prick ears while others like drop ears. Most show dogs have erect ears.

◀ SKYE TERRIER

This breed was developed in Britain more than 400 years ago. It is a solid dog which weighs up to 25 pounds and stands 10 inches. It has a hard coat which hangs more than 5 inches from the body, straight down. It is available in both drop and prick ears but most breeders prefer the prick ears.

It appears in black, gray, fawn or cream.

SOFT COATED WHEATEN TERRIER ▶

This lovely Irish dog reaches 35 pounds and 19 inches. It has a coat which is thick, soft and silky (thus the name *soft coated*). It is found in colors from light wheaten to golden red with wheaten, of course, the preferred color. Show grooming requires skill and experience. Constant brushing is required to prevent hairs from building up all over the house, but brushing is easy and enjoyable for most dogs and it removes all of the loose hairs if properly done.

Staffordshire Bull Terrier

STAFFORDSHIRE BULL TERRIER ➤

This dog originated in Britain. It grows to 38 pounds at a height of 16 inches. This was the original cross of the Bull-and-Terrier produced in the late 1700s. It has a short, smooth coat and occurs in red, fawn, white, black, blue and brindle with or without white markings. It requires firm and patient training as a pup or he'll be dragging you down the street when you have him on a lead. He was used as a pit bull and is a born fighter so don't let him get involved with others dogs or he likely will injure them.

The Staffordshire Bull Terrier is more popular in England today than it is in America. In America, a similar but larger dog exists in the American Staffordshire Terrier, which is sometimes called the American Pit Bull Terrier. Despite the bad press of recent years, all of these breeds are friendly and good with children— JUST NOT OTHER DOGS.

Standard Schnauzer

◀ STANDARD SCHNAUZER
This German dog weighs about 33 pounds at slightly under 20 inches. It salt and pepper or black coat is wiry and rough. It is a true terrier with the ratter instincts and, because of its size, has also been utilized as a drover's dog, stock tender and guard dog both for humans and animals.

In Germany, Standard Schnauzers are still used on farms where they are kept busy constantly. These dogs are easily bored; if you don't have time for them, don't acquire one. The Standard Schnauzer has a very limited following in the USA, and this is true in England too. Even on the Continent the breed is not terribly numerous. Most dog people regard the breed important because of its role in dog history and breed evolution.

SUSSEX SPANIEL ▶

This dog originated in Great Britain where it is shown at a maximum of 45 pounds and 15.5 inches in height. Its flat, silky, long coat may be solid golden liver with no white spots on the chest. Such a mark is faulty. This is a gun dog and is selectively used for hunting.

◀ TIBETAN SPANIEL

This dog originated in China. It reaches a height of 10 inches and a weight of 9 to 15 pounds. This dog was raised in monasteries and was used for various tasks. The monks made them into wonderful pets which were selectively bred for their personality. The monks carried them under their robes to stay warm.

TIBETAN TERRIER ▶

This dog originated in Tibet. It reaches 30 pounds and 16 inches and was once used for herding and guard duty. It has a long, shaggy coat that covers its face. The coat colors are white, gray, black, or golden, with or without white or tan. In order to keep this dog in show condition, a huge amount of time and skill is necessary to maintain its coat.

These dogs were brought into Europe by the Magyars (Hungarians) hundreds of years ago. Hungarian language and Tibetan language have many similarities while Hungarian has almost no resemblance to any European language except, perhaps, Finnish. The Magyars used this dog to develop their own Puli as it is similar in size, shape, tail carriage and working characteristics.

Toy Fox Terrier

TOY FOX TERRIER ▶

This American breed is well known because it is the ideal dog for travelling magicians. This little rascal has a short, smooth coat requiring almost no attention, doesn't eat much, can easily be hidden in a hotel room—this is the least costly of all intelligent dogs for a travelling magician to have. It weighs from 3.5 to 7 pounds and stays under 10 inches tall. It is usually tricolored as tan, black and white and is sometimes sold as an AmerToy. His natural instincts are to be a clown so he loves the theater, even if it's only in your living room.

◀ VIZSLA

This breed originated in Hungary where it reaches 62 pounds at 2 feet tall. It may be shorthaired or wirehaired and must be various shades of gold. It is a gun dog and is used extensively for hunting. It is extremely intelligent and is often seen in obedience competitions. This was an old breed in Hungary, perhaps as old as 500 years, but it has only been in the USA and UK since the 1930s or thereabouts.

WEIMARANER ▶

This dog originated in Germany where it is only found in light gray, with short fine hair for the shorthaired variety, or 2 inch long hair in the longhaired variety. It is the ultimate gundog according to those people who hunt with them. The shorthaired variety has its tail docked but the longhair has an undocked tail. Only shortcoated dogs can be exhibited in the USA.

Welsh Springer Spaniel

WELSH SPRINGER SPANIEL ➡

   This dog originated in Great Britain and reaches 45 pounds in weight. It has a straight flat coat with significant feathering. It is only recognized in red/white combination. This breed has been made famous by Victorian Welsh painters who featured these gun dogs in their works of art. These are nice pets and good hunting dogs, too.

Welsh Terrier

WELSH TERRIER ◆

This dog originated in Great Britain where it weighs in at 20 pounds at 15 inches high. It has a black/tan wire coat and is a true terrier. Just looking at his beautiful face shows his curiosity, intelligence and playfulness. He must be carefully trained as a puppy or you will have your hands full! They are especially fond of children and the water.

Whippet

◀ WEST HIGHLAND WHITE TERRIER

This is an English breed that reaches 22 pounds at under 12 inches. It has a rough, wiry white coat and is a typical terrier. They are bouncy, over-friendly and courageous, and wonderful pets if properly trained when they are puppies.

WHIPPET ▶ ➡

The Whippet is a British breed which reaches 28 pounds at 22 inches at the shoulder. They come in every dog color and were bred to be the race horse of the common man.

Speed is the Whippet's goal and it is not unusual for them to run at 35 miles per hour and to cover 200 yards in 12 seconds. They also make great pets and their underslung tail and drooped ears, normally a sign of surrender, is normal for them. A long-haired variety has recently been promoted. It has been rejected by the AKC in favor of the normal short, fine, close coat which is so familiar.

Wirehaired Pointing Griffon

WIREHAIRED POINTING GRIFFON ☛

This dog was produced in France where it reaches 50 pounds at 2 feet in height at the shoulder. They look larger. Their coat is coarse and hard and their beard and eyebrows are a must. The usual colors are solid chestnut, or chestnut with white or steel gray markings. This is a real hunting dog which makes a fine pet and house dog if you give him lots of love, training and exercise. His rough coat needs little attention.

Yorkshire Terrier

YORKSHIRE TERRIER ◄

This breed originated in Great Britain. It is a toy terrier...a lap dog, which stays under 9 inches and under 7 pounds in weight. However, the world's smallest dog was a Yorkie of 10 ounces. Even though tiny, they are sharp and typically terrier, chasing small animals and being nasty to strangers. I once tried to pet a small Yorkie sitting in his mistress's lap and no sooner did my hand get over his head...*SNAP*..and my hand was bleeding. The army tells stories of these small dogs carrying a wire through a long, 8 inch pipe. It's a nice dog if you want a lap dog, but the grooming is a daily must.

BOOKS ABOUT DOGS

Your pet shop has access to a dog book on hundreds of dog breeds. You can order any TFH Publications book through your local pet shop.

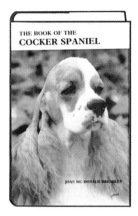
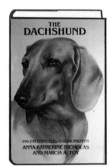
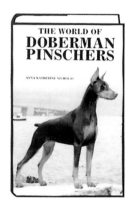

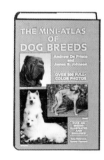

BOOKS ABOUT DOGS

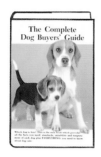

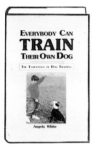

BOOKS ABOUT DOGS

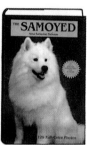
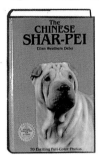

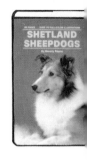

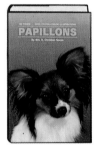

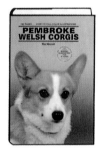

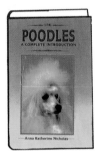

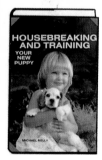

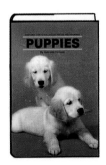